CBEST Prep Book 2023-2024

Master the CBEST Exam with In-Depth Content Review of Reading, Writing, and Math Section | Exam Strategies, Full-Length Practice Tests with Detailed Answer Explanations

Test Treasure Publication

COPYRIGHT

Unauthorized use or duplication of this material without express and written permission from this site's owner and/or author is strictly prohibited. Excerpts and links may be used, provided that full and clear credit is given to Test Treasure Publication with appropriate and specific direction to the original content.

Trademarks

All trademarks, service marks, and trade names used within this website and Test Treasure Publication's products are proprietary to Test Treasure Publication or other respective owners that have granted Test Treasure Publication the right and license to use such intellectual property.

Disclaimer

While every effort has been made to ensure the accuracy and completeness of the information contained in our products, Test Treasure Publication assumes no responsibility for errors, omissions, or contradictory interpretation of the subject matter herein. All information is provided "as is" without warranty of any kind.

Governing Law

This website is controlled by Test Treasure Publication from our offices located in the state of California, USA. It can be accessed by most countries around the world. As each country has laws that may differ from those of California, by accessing our website, you agree that the statutes and laws of California, without regard to the conflict of laws and the United Nations Convention on the International Sales of Goods, will apply to all matters relating to the use of this website and the purchase of any products or services through this site.

CONTENTS

Introduction

Your Gateway to Success in the California Basic Educational Skills Test

Welcome to the definitive guide for conquering the California Basic Educational Skills Test (CBEST) in 2023-2024! Published by Test Treasure Publication, this comprehensive resource is designed to be your trusted companion on the journey to excellence.

Unveiling the Path to Success

Understanding the Exam Landscape

Embark on your CBEST preparation journey with a clear understanding of the exam's intricacies. In this guide, we unveil the exam pattern, administered body, time frame, and, most importantly, the significance of CBEST in shaping your educational and professional future.

Navigating the Sections

A Deep Dive into Reading, Writing, and Mathematics

Dive into the core of CBEST with detailed content reviews for each section. Whether it's mastering Critical Analysis and Evaluation in Reading, crafting compelling Personal Experience Essays in Writing, or tackling complex Estimation and Problem Solving in Mathematics, we've got you covered.

Your Personalized Study Companion

Schedules, FAQs, and Strategies

Navigate through meticulously crafted study schedules and planning advice tailored to optimize your preparation. Find answers to frequently asked questions, and unlock test-taking strategies that go beyond the ordinary, ensuring you approach each section with confidence.

Practice Makes Perfect

Two Full-Length Practice Tests

Put your knowledge to the test with not one, but two full-length practice tests. With 100 questions each, accompanied by detailed answer explanations, these simulations provide the perfect opportunity to fine-tune your skills and gauge your readiness for the CBEST.

Beyond the Book

Recommended Resources for Continued Excellence

Discover a curated list of online resources and academic materials that complement your preparation, extending your learning beyond the pages of this book. Maximize your potential with additional tools handpicked for your success.

A Final Word of Encouragement

Empowering You for Success

As you navigate through the pages of "CBEST Prep Book 2023-2024," let the final words serve as a source of motivation. Success in the CBEST is not just a destination; it's a transformative journey toward a future filled with boundless opportunities.

Join us at Test Treasure Publication, where your success story begins. Illuminate your path to extraordinary success with "CBEST Prep Book 2023-2024."

Brief Overview of the CBEST Exam

Exam Pattern:

The California Basic Educational Skills Test (CBEST) is a standardized test designed to assess basic proficiency in reading, writing, and mathematics. The exam consists of three sections:

1. **Reading**: Evaluate critical analysis, comprehension, and research skills.

2. **Writing**: Assess personal and analytical essay writing abilities.

3. **Mathematics**: Measure estimation, computation, problem-solving, and numerical/graphic relationship skills.

Number of Questions:

Each section of the CBEST exam contains multiple-choice questions. The total number of questions may vary slightly from one administration to another but typically falls within the following ranges:

- Reading: Approximately 50 questions

- Writing: Approximately 50 questions

- Mathematics: Approximately 50 questions

Time:

Candidates are allotted a total of four hours to complete all sections of the CBEST exam. The time distribution among the sections may vary, but typically candidates have around 1 hour and 15 minutes for each section.

Score:

The CBEST exam is scored on a scale of 20 to 80 for each section, with a passing score of 41 required for each section. The total passing score for all three sections combined is 123.

Administered By:

The CBEST exam is administered by the California Commission on Teacher Credentialing (CTC), the state agency responsible for setting standards for teacher certification and credentialing in California.

Importance:

The CBEST exam is a crucial step for individuals seeking to pursue a career in education in California. A passing score on the CBEST is required for admission to teacher preparation programs, as well as for obtaining a teaching credential or certification in the state. Additionally, many school districts and educational institutions use CBEST scores as part of their hiring criteria for teachers and educators.

DETAILED CONTENT REVIEW

Section 1: Reading

1.1 Critical Analysis and Evaluation

Uncover the Art of Evaluation

- **Evaluate Content:** Develop the skills to critically analyze and evaluate content. Understand how to assess the validity, reliability, and relevance of information.

- **Identify Logical Fallacies:** Hone your ability to identify logical fallacies within written passages. Strengthen your critical thinking to distinguish sound reasoning from flawed arguments.

1.2 Comprehension and Research Skills

Mastering Comprehension

- **Identifying Main Ideas:** Sharpen your comprehension skills by identifying main ideas within complex texts. Learn effective strategies to extract key information efficiently.

- **Recognizing Supporting Details:** Navigate through passages with precision, recognizing and interpreting supporting details. Develop a keen eye for the nuances that shape the overall meaning.

Section 2: Writing

2.1 Personal Experience Essay

Crafting Compelling Narratives

- **Narrative Structure:** Learn the art of crafting a compelling personal experience essay. Understand the nuances of narrative structure to engage your readers effectively.

- **Emotional Appeal and Descriptive Elements:** Elevate your writing with emotional appeal and vivid descriptive elements. Create narratives that resonate with authenticity and evoke a strong connection.

2.2 Analytical Essay

Mastering Analytical Writing

- **Thesis Development:** Unlock the secrets of effective thesis development. Craft a clear and compelling thesis statement that forms the backbone of your analytical essays.

- **Logical Reasoning and Evidence:** Dive into the world of logical reasoning and evidence presentation. Develop the skills to build a coherent argument supported by relevant and convincing evidence.

Section 3: Mathematics

3.1 Estimation, Measurement, and Statistical Principles

Navigating the Mathematical Landscape

- **Approximations:** Master the art of making accurate approximations. Strengthen your estimation skills to tackle real-world problems effectively.

- **Data Interpretation:** Develop proficiency in interpreting data presented in various formats. Enhance your ability to extract meaningful insights from tables, graphs, and charts.

3.2 Computation and Problem Solving

Mathematical Prowess Unleashed

- **Arithmetic Calculations:** Refine your arithmetic skills with a focus on speed and accuracy. Tackle mathematical problems with confidence, utilizing efficient computation techniques.

- **Algebraic Equations:** Demystify algebraic equations with clear and concise explanations. Learn problem-solving strategies to approach algebraic challenges with ease.

3.3 Numerical and Graphic Relationships

Understanding Mathematical Relations

- **Mathematical Relations:** Explore the intricate relationships between numbers. Develop a deep understanding of mathematical concepts to tackle questions involving numerical relationships.

- **Reading Graphs and Tables:** Navigate through graphical representations with proficiency. Learn to extract meaningful information from graphs and tables to solve numerical problems.

Two Full-Length Practice Tests

Simulate Real Exam Conditions

Put your knowledge to the test with two full-length practice tests, each comprising 100 questions. Detailed answer explanations accompany each question, providing valuable insights to enhance your understanding.

Additional Resources

Recommended Online Resources and Academic Materials

Discover a curated list of online resources and academic materials that complement your preparation. Expand your learning beyond the book and access tools that enrich your knowledge base.

Final Words

A Source of Motivation

The journey to success doesn't end with the exam. Find a final word of encouragement that resonates with your aspirations. Let these motivating words inspire you to embrace the opportunities that await you.

STUDY SCHEDULES AND PLANNING ADVICE

Crafting Your Path to Success

Embarking on the journey to conquer the CBEST requires not just knowledge but a strategic plan. In this section, we provide you with meticulously crafted study schedules and invaluable planning advice to optimize your preparation and enhance your chances of success.

Study Schedules

Tailored to Your Needs

Our study schedules are designed with your busy life in mind. Whether you have a few months or just weeks to prepare, find schedules that align with your timeframe, allowing you to cover the material thoroughly while minimizing stress.

Weekly Breakdown

Each schedule provides a weekly breakdown, outlining the topics and sections to focus on during the week. This organized approach ensures you cover all necessary content without feeling overwhelmed.

Flexibility Built-In

Recognizing the unpredictability of life, our schedules come with built-in flexibility. Life happens, and we understand that. Adjust the schedule as needed, ensuring that you stay on track while accommodating your personal commitments.

Planning Advice

Setting Realistic Goals

Understand the power of setting realistic and achievable goals. Break down your study sessions into manageable tasks, creating a sense of accomplishment with each milestone reached.

Balancing Sections

CBEST assesses multiple skills, and our planning advice guides you on how to balance your focus across Reading, Writing, and Mathematics. Create a harmonious study plan that allows you to excel in each section.

Practice Tests Integration

Incorporate the two full-length practice tests strategically into your schedule. Simulate exam conditions to enhance your time management and build endurance for the actual test day.

Review and Reflection

Regularly review your progress and reflect on your strengths and areas for improvement. Adjust your study plan based on this feedback, ensuring continuous growth throughout your preparation.

Pro Tips

Time Management Techniques

Master the art of time management with our expert tips. Learn techniques to optimize your study sessions, making the most of every moment and maximizing your retention of critical information.

Stress Reduction Strategies

CBEST preparation can be intense, but our guide includes stress reduction strategies to keep you focused and calm. Cultivate a positive mindset, and approach the exam with confidence and clarity.

Your Personalized Success Plan

Crafting a successful study plan is not just about the quantity of study hours but the quality of your preparation. With our study schedules and planning advice, you're not just preparing for an exam; you're crafting a path to success that aligns with your unique strengths and goals.

FREQUENTLY ASKED QUESTIONS

Q1: What makes "CBEST Prep Book 2023-2024" unique?

Answer: Our book stands out with its comprehensive coverage of CBEST content, personalized study schedules, and strategic planning advice. It goes beyond being a traditional study guide; it's your mentor on the journey to CBEST success.

Q2: How can I use the study schedules effectively?

Answer: The study schedules are crafted to suit different timelines. Choose a schedule that aligns with your available preparation time, and follow the weekly breakdown to cover all sections efficiently. Don't forget to incorporate flexibility based on your unique schedule.

Q3: Are the practice tests reflective of the actual CBEST exam?

Answer: Absolutely! The two full-length practice tests are designed to simulate real exam conditions. They cover a range of question types and difficulty levels, providing you with a comprehensive assessment of your readiness for the CBEST.

Q4: How do I balance preparation for the Reading, Writing, and Mathematics sections?

Answer: Our planning advice guides you in balancing your focus across all sections. It's about creating a harmonious study plan that allows you to excel in each area. The weekly breakdown in the study schedules also helps you allocate time effectively.

Q5: Can I adjust the study schedules to fit my personal commitments?

Answer: Absolutely! Life can be unpredictable, and our study schedules come with built-in flexibility. Adjust the schedule as needed, ensuring that you stay on track while accommodating your personal and professional commitments.

Q6: How can I manage stress during my CBEST preparation?

Answer: Our guide includes stress reduction strategies to help you maintain focus and clarity. Techniques for time management and positive mindset cultivation contribute to a balanced and stress-free preparation journey.

Q7: Are the recommended online resources and academic materials essential?

Answer: While the book provides comprehensive content, the additional resources serve as supplements to enrich your learning. They are recommended to enhance your understanding and provide additional practice opportunities.

Q8: What is the significance of the Final Words section?

Answer: The Final Words section serves as a source of motivation. It inspires you to see beyond the exam, encouraging you to embrace the opportunities that come with success. It's a reminder that your journey doesn't end with the test; it's a stepping stone to a fulfilling future.

Q9: Can I use this book for last-minute preparation?

Answer: Yes, our study schedules include options for both extended and last-minute preparation. Follow the condensed schedules for effective last-minute review, focusing on key concepts and practice tests.

Q10: How can I track my progress throughout the preparation?

Answer: Regularly review your progress using the reflection prompts in the planning advice section. Assess your strengths and areas for improvement, and adjust your study plan accordingly for continuous growth.

SECTION 1: READING

Critical Analysis and Evaluation

1. Evaluate Content

Unraveling Depth: Understanding Content in Depth

Welcome to the first chapter of Section 1: Reading—where we embark on a journey into the depths of critical analysis and evaluation of written content. Reading is not merely about scanning words; it's about understanding, discerning, and evaluating the richness of information presented in passages.

Why is this important?

The ability to evaluate content is a skill that goes beyond the surface level. It involves dissecting written material, understanding the author's intent, and critically assessing the depth of the information. This skill is not only crucial for success in the CBEST but also for real-world scenarios where critical analysis is key.

Key Concepts:

1. **Depth Perception:** Learn to discern the layers of meaning within a passage. Understand how to identify and interpret subtle nuances that

contribute to the overall message.

2. **Relevance Assessment:** Practice evaluating the relevance of information. Distinguish between central themes and peripheral details to focus on the most critical aspects of the text.

3. **Discerning Key Concepts:** Sharpen your ability to recognize and extract key concepts. Identify the core ideas that shape the passage and contribute to the author's main message.

Practical Application:

Engage in exercises that involve reading passages from various genres. Apply the skills learned to evaluate the depth of content, asking questions such as:

- What is the primary message of the passage?

- How does the author support their main idea?

- What layers of meaning can be extracted from the text?

By the end of this chapter, you will not only read but truly understand the content at a profound level.

2. Identify Logical Fallacies

Navigating Flawed Reasoning: Sharpening Analytical Skills

Logical fallacies can be stumbling blocks in understanding written content. In this chapter, we focus on identifying and navigating through these pitfalls, sharpening your analytical skills to approach passages with a discerning eye.

Why is this important?

Logical fallacies are errors in reasoning that can distort the intended message of a passage. Being able to identify these flaws is crucial for maintaining clarity in comprehension. It's about reading critically and recognizing when an argument may be weak or misleading.

Key Concepts:

1. **Flawed Reasoning Patterns:** Explore common logical fallacies such as ad hominem attacks, straw man arguments, and hasty generalizations. Understand how these patterns can appear in written material.

2. **Identifying Faulty Arguments:** Develop the ability to spot flawed arguments and reasoning. Learn to question the validity of statements and conclusions presented in the text.

3. **Critical Reading Strategies:** Cultivate strategies for reading with a critical eye. Practice pausing to evaluate the logic behind the author's statements and identifying potential pitfalls.

Practical Application:

Engage in exercises that present passages containing logical fallacies. Analyze the text, highlighting instances of flawed reasoning. Discuss and debate these examples to reinforce your understanding of logical pitfalls.

By the end of this chapter, you'll not only be a proficient reader but a critical thinker capable of navigating through complex arguments with ease.

Comprehension and Research Skills

1. Identifying Main Ideas

Grasping the Core: Understanding Main Ideas

The ability to identify main ideas is foundational for effective reading comprehension. This chapter focuses on honing your skills in recognizing and grasping the core concepts presented in passages.

Why is this important?

Main ideas serve as the backbone of any written piece. Being able to identify and understand these central themes is essential for comprehensive comprehension. It allows you to extract the essence of the passage and grasp the author's primary message.

Key Concepts:

1. **Central Themes:** Learn to distinguish central themes from supporting details. Understand how to identify the overarching ideas that shape the passage.

2. **Focus on Significance:** Practice discerning the significance of main ideas. Develop the ability to recognize which concepts carry the most weight in conveying the author's intended message.

3. **Synthesizing Information:** Cultivate the skill of synthesizing information. Connect main ideas across paragraphs to create a cohesive understanding of the entire passage.

Practical Application:

Engage in exercises that present passages with clear main ideas. Practice identifying and summarizing these central themes. Explore how main ideas connect and contribute to the overall coherence of the text.

By the end of this chapter, you'll have a heightened ability to identify and understand the core concepts that shape written material.

2. Recognizing Supporting Details

The Power of Details: Enhancing Comprehension

In this chapter, we delve into the importance of supporting details and how they enrich the overall comprehension of a passage. Recognizing and understanding these details is key to extracting the full meaning from written material.

Why is this important?

Supporting details provide depth and context to main ideas. They offer evidence, examples, and nuances that contribute to a comprehensive understanding of the passage. Being able to recognize and interpret these details enhances your overall comprehension skills.

Key Concepts:

1. **Evaluating Relevance:** Practice evaluating the relevance of supporting details. Understand how to distinguish between essential and peripheral information.

2. **Contextual Understanding:** Develop the ability to understand the context provided by supporting details. Identify how these details contribute to the overall meaning of the passage.

3. **Connecting Main Ideas and Details:** Cultivate strategies for connecting main ideas with supporting details. Recognize how these elements work together to convey the author's message.

Practical Application:

Engage in exercises that focus on passages with intricate supporting details. Practice extracting and interpreting these details to build a comprehensive understanding of the text.

By the end of this chapter, you'll be adept at recognizing the power of details and utilizing them to enhance your overall comprehension skills.

SECTION 2: WRITING

Personal Experience Essay

1. Narrative Structure

Crafting Compelling Narratives: The Art of Storytelling

Welcome to the first chapter of Section 2: Writing—where we explore the intricacies of crafting a powerful personal experience essay through effective narrative structure. Writing is not just about conveying information; it's about telling a story that captivates and resonates with your audience.

Why is this important?

The personal experience essay allows you to showcase your unique perspective and connect with readers on a personal level. Understanding narrative structure is key to presenting your experiences in a compelling and engaging manner.

Key Concepts:

1. **Introduction to Narrative Elements:** Explore the fundamental elements of a narrative, including characters, setting, plot, and theme. Understand how these elements contribute to the overall structure of your essay.

2. **Creating a Story Arc:** Learn to develop a story arc that takes readers on a journey. Craft a compelling beginning, build tension in the middle, and provide a satisfying resolution.

3. **Showcasing Personal Growth:** Understand how to use your experiences to convey personal growth. Explore techniques for reflecting on your journey and expressing the lessons learned.

Practical Application:

Engage in exercises that involve crafting short narratives. Practice incorporating narrative elements into your writing and experiment with different story structures. Receive feedback to refine your ability to construct compelling narratives.

By the end of this chapter, you'll be equipped with the skills to transform your personal experiences into captivating stories.

2. Emotional Appeal and Descriptive Elements

Evoking Emotions through Detail: The Power of Description

In this chapter, we delve into the art of infusing emotion into your personal experience essay. Emotional appeal, coupled with vivid descriptive elements, creates a powerful connection with your readers, making your writing memorable and impactful.

Why is this important?

Emotions are a universal language that resonates with readers. By incorporating emotional appeal and vivid descriptions, you create a sensory experience for your audience, immersing them in your narrative.

Key Concepts:

1. **Tapping into Emotions:** Explore techniques for tapping into and expressing emotions authentically. Understand how emotions contribute to the overall impact of your writing.

2. **Creating Vivid Imagery:** Develop the skill of creating vivid imagery through descriptive elements. Paint a picture with your words, allowing readers to visualize and experience your narrative.

3. **Balancing Detail and Impact:** Learn to strike a balance between detailed descriptions and maintaining the impact of your narrative. Understand when and how to use descriptive elements effectively.

Practical Application:

Engage in exercises that focus on evoking specific emotions through your writing. Experiment with different descriptive techniques and receive feedback on the emotional impact of your narratives.

By the end of this chapter, you'll be adept at infusing your personal experience essay with emotional depth and captivating descriptions.

Analytical Essay

1. Thesis Development

Crafting Clear and Concise Arguments: The Art of Thesis Development

Welcome to the first chapter of the Analytical Essay section—where we explore the foundational skill of crafting a clear and concise thesis. The thesis is the backbone of your analytical essay, providing a roadmap for your readers and guiding the development of your arguments.

Why is this important?

A well-developed thesis sets the tone for your analytical essay. It not only articulates the main point but also outlines the direction of your arguments. Understanding how to craft a strong thesis is essential for presenting a compelling and organized analysis.

Key Concepts:

1. **Defining the Thesis:** Understand the role of the thesis in an analytical essay. Explore different types of theses, including argumentative, explanatory, and analytical.

2. **Clarity and Precision:** Learn to articulate your thesis with clarity and precision. Avoid vague or broad statements and focus on presenting a concise and specific argument.

3. **Connecting to Arguments:** Explore how the thesis serves as a guide for developing arguments. Understand the relationship between the thesis statement and the overall structure of your essay.

Practical Application:

Engage in exercises that involve crafting and refining thesis statements for analytical prompts. Receive feedback on the clarity and effectiveness of your theses.

By the end of this chapter, you'll possess the skills to develop a compelling thesis that forms the foundation of your analytical essay.

2. Logical Reasoning and Evidence

Building a Persuasive Argument: The Role of Logic and Evidence

In this chapter, we explore the intricacies of building a persuasive argument through logical reasoning and the effective use of evidence. Your analytical essay relies on the strength of your arguments and the evidence that supports them.

Why is this important?

Logical reasoning and evidence are the pillars of a persuasive analytical essay. They lend credibility to your arguments, convincing your readers of the validity of your analysis. Understanding how to build a coherent and well-supported argument is essential for success.

Key Concepts:

1. **Logical Structure:** Explore the principles of logical reasoning in constructing arguments. Understand how to arrange ideas coherently and establish a logical flow in your essay.

2. **Types of Evidence:** Learn to identify and incorporate different types of evidence, including statistical data, examples, anecdotes, and expert opinions. Understand the strengths and weaknesses of each.

3. **Evaluating Credibility:** Develop the skill of evaluating the credibility of evidence sources. Understand how to discern reliable and authoritative sources to strengthen your arguments.

Practical Application:

Engage in exercises that involve building arguments based on specific prompts. Practice selecting and integrating evidence to support your claims. Receive feedback on the logical flow and persuasiveness of your arguments.

By the end of this chapter, you'll be proficient in constructing persuasive arguments through logical reasoning and compelling evidence.

SECTION 3: MATHEMATICS

1. Estimation, Measurement, and Statistical Principles

Approximations

Welcome to the first chapter of Section 3: Mathematics—where we explore the critical concepts of estimation and approximations. Developing a strong foundation in approximating values is essential for tackling mathematical problems with confidence and precision.

Why is this important?

Estimation is not just about making quick guesses; it's a strategic skill that helps you navigate complex mathematical problems. Understanding how to make accurate approximations lays the groundwork for successful problem-solving in various mathematical scenarios.

Key Concepts:

1. **Introduction to Approximations:** Understand the fundamental principles of estimation and how it differs from precise calculation. Explore real-world scenarios where approximations are valuable.

2. **Strategies for Mental Math:** Learn mental math techniques for making quick and accurate approximations. Discover shortcuts and tricks to

simplify complex calculations on-the-fly.

3. **Applications in Problem Solving:** Apply approximation skills to solve practical problems in different mathematical domains. Develop the ability to assess when and how to use approximations effectively.

Practical Application:

Engage in exercises that involve real-life scenarios where estimation is crucial. Practice making quick approximations and refine your mental math skills through hands-on problem-solving.

By the end of this chapter, you'll be equipped with the skills to make precise approximations, a valuable asset in the CBEST Mathematics section.

Data Interpretation

Moving on to the second aspect of this chapter, we delve into the realm of data interpretation. The ability to extract meaningful insights from data sets is an essential skill for the CBEST Mathematics section.

Why is this important?

In today's data-driven world, interpreting information presented in various formats is a critical skill. Whether it's graphs, tables, or charts, being able to extract relevant data and draw conclusions is fundamental to success.

Key Concepts:

1. **Types of Data Representations:** Explore common types of data representations, including bar graphs, line graphs, pie charts, and tables. Understand the strengths and limitations of each.

2. **Analyzing Trends and Patterns:** Learn to identify trends, patterns,

and anomalies within data sets. Develop the ability to draw conclusions and make informed decisions based on data interpretation.

3. **Practical Applications:** Apply data interpretation skills to solve mathematical problems relevant to the CBEST exam. Practice extracting information from various representations and using it to answer questions.

Practical Application:

Engage in exercises that involve interpreting data from different sources. Practice analyzing graphs, tables, and charts to extract relevant information and solve mathematical problems.

By the end of this chapter, you'll have honed your data interpretation skills, a crucial aspect of success in the CBEST Mathematics section.

2. Computation and Problem Solving

Arithmetic Calculations

Welcome to the first chapter of the Computation and Problem Solving section, where we delve into essential arithmetic calculations. Building a strong foundation in arithmetic lays the groundwork for tackling more complex mathematical problems with confidence.

Why is this important?

Arithmetic is the cornerstone of mathematics, and a solid grasp of basic calculations is essential for success in the CBEST exam. Whether it's addition, subtraction, multiplication, or division, mastering these fundamental operations is crucial.

Key Concepts:

1. **Review of Basic Operations:** Refresh your understanding of addition, subtraction, multiplication, and division. Explore common pitfalls and strategies for minimizing errors in calculations.

2. **Order of Operations:** Understand the importance of the order of operations in solving mathematical problems. Learn how to approach multi-step problems with precision.

3. **Speed and Accuracy:** Develop techniques for improving both speed and accuracy in arithmetic calculations. Practice mental math exercises to enhance your computational skills.

Practical Application:

Engage in exercises that involve a variety of arithmetic calculations. Practice solving problems with different levels of complexity to reinforce your mastery of basic operations.

By the end of this chapter, you'll have strengthened your foundation in arithmetic, a crucial component of success in the CBEST Mathematics section.

Algebraic Equations

Moving on to the second aspect of this chapter, we explore the realm of algebraic equations. Algebraic equations form the basis for solving a wide range of mathematical problems, making them a key focus for the CBEST exam.

Why is this important?

Algebraic equations provide a powerful tool for problem-solving, allowing you to represent relationships between variables and find solutions to complex problems. Understanding how to set up and solve algebraic equations is fundamental to success in the CBEST Mathematics section.

Key Concepts:

1. **Introduction to Algebraic Expressions:** Review the basics of algebraic expressions, including variables, constants, and coefficients. Understand how to translate real-world problems into algebraic equations.

2. **Solving Linear Equations:** Learn systematic approaches to solving linear equations. Explore different methods, including the balance method and inverse operations.

3. **Practical Applications:** Apply algebraic equation-solving skills to solve problems relevant to the CBEST exam. Practice translating word problems into equations and finding solutions.

Practical Application:

Engage in exercises that involve solving a variety of algebraic equations. Practice identifying variables, setting up equations, and finding solutions to reinforce your algebraic problem-solving skills.

By the end of this chapter, you'll be well-equipped to tackle algebraic equations confidently in the CBEST Mathematics section.

3. Numerical and Graphic Relationships

Mathematical Relations

In this chapter, we explore the concept of mathematical relations—an essential component of understanding numerical and graphic relationships. Developing proficiency in recognizing and interpreting relations is key to success in the CBEST Mathematics section.

Why is this important?

Mathematical relations form the basis for understanding how variables interact and influence each other. Whether presented in numerical or graphic form, recognizing these relationships is crucial for solving problems and making informed decisions.

Key Concepts:

1. **Defining Mathematical Relations:** Understand the concept of mathematical relations and how they represent connections between variables. Explore different types of relations, including direct and inverse.

2. **Interpreting Graphical Representations:** Learn to interpret graphs that represent mathematical relations. Understand how to identify trends, patterns, and key features in graphical representations.

3. **Applications in Problem Solving:** Apply knowledge of mathematical relations to solve problems relevant to the CBEST exam. Practice identifying and using relations to answer questions and make predictions.

Practical Application:

Engage in exercises that involve analyzing numerical and graphical representations of mathematical relations. Practice identifying key features and using them to solve problems.

By the end of this chapter, you'll have honed your skills in recognizing and interpreting mathematical relations, a crucial aspect of success in the CBEST Mathematics section.

Reading Graphs and Tables

Moving on to the second aspect of this chapter, we focus specifically on reading graphs and tables. Proficiency in interpreting graphical representations is vital for tackling mathematical problems effectively.

Why is this important?

Graphs and tables convey complex information in a visual format. Being able to extract relevant data, identify trends, and draw conclusions from these representations is an essential skill for success in the CBEST Mathematics section.

Key Concepts:

1. **Types of Graphs and Tables:** Explore different types of graphs, including line graphs, bar graphs, and pie charts. Understand the structure of tables and how to extract information effectively.

2. **Analyzing Trends and Patterns:** Learn to identify trends and patterns in graphical representations. Understand how to use graphs and tables to answer specific questions and solve mathematical problems.

3. **Practical Applications:** Apply skills in reading graphs and tables to solve problems relevant to the CBEST exam. Practice extracting information and making calculations based on graphical data.

Practical Application:

Engage in exercises that involve interpreting various graphs and tables. Practice analyzing data presented in visual formats and using it to answer questions and solve mathematical problems.

4.1 FULL-LENGTH PRACTICE TEST 1

Section 1: Reading

1. Evaluate Content

Question 1: The main argument of a passage states that fast food is a major contributor to obesity. Which of the following statements would weaken this argument?

A) Fast food is convenient and cheap.

B) Many people who eat fast food are not obese.

C) Fast food companies are major job providers.

D) Exercise is also important for controlling weight.

2. Identify Logical Fallacies

Question 2: Which of the following is an example of an ad hominem attack?

A) Your argument is invalid because you never went to college.

B) Your argument is invalid because it has internal contradictions.

C) Your argument is invalid because it is not popular.

D) Your argument is invalid because it's too complex.

3. Identifying Main Ideas

Question 3: What is the main idea of a passage that discusses the environmental impact of plastic waste?

A) Plastic is convenient

B) Plastic waste harms marine life

C) Recycling is important

D) Plastic is cheap

4. Recognizing Supporting Details

Question 4: In a passage about renewable energy, which of the following would be a supporting detail?

A) Solar energy is abundant

B) Energy is important

C) Coal is outdated

D) Cars use gas

Section 2: Writing

5. Narrative Structure

Question 5: In a narrative essay, the _____ introduces the setting, characters, and basic situation.

A) Climax

B) Resolution

C) Exposition

D) Rising Action

6. Emotional Appeal and Descriptive Elements

Question 6: Which of the following elements can add emotional depth to a personal experience essay?

A) Statistics

B) Dialogue

C) Jargon

D) Bullet points

7. Thesis Development

Question 7: A good thesis statement should be:

A) Vague

B) Specific

C) Lengthy

D) A question

8. Logical Reasoning and Evidence

Question 8: Which of the following should not be used as evidence in an analytical essay?

A) Personal opinions

B) Scientific studies

C) Expert testimony

D) Statistical data

Section 3: Mathematics

9. Approximations

Question 9: If π is approximately 3.14159, what is π rounded to the nearest whole number?

A) 3

B) 4

C) 0

D) 1

10. Data Interpretation

Question 10: If a bar graph shows that 30% of a class prefers chocolate, what can be inferred?

A) No one likes vanilla

B) 70% prefer other flavors

C) Chocolate is healthy

D) The class is large

11. Arithmetic Calculations

Question 11: What is 25×4?

A) 50

B) 100

C) 200

D) 125

12. Algebraic Equations

Question 12: What is the value of x in the equation $2x=10$?

A) 2

B) 5

C) 10

D) 20

13. Mathematical Relations

Question 13: If $a=b$, then $a^2=$?

A) b^2

B) $2b$

C) a

D) b

14. Reading Graphs and Tables

Question 14: In a line graph that shows temperature over a week, if the line is descending, what does that mean?

A) The temperature is constant

B) The temperature is rising

C) The temperature is falling

D) The graph is incorrect

Section 1: Reading

15. Evaluate Content

Question 15: Which of the following is a strong counter-argument against the statement "All video games are harmful to children"?

A) Some video games improve hand-eye coordination

B) Video games are fun

C) Kids love video games

D) Video games are popular

16. Identify Logical Fallacies

Question 16: Which of the following statements is a red herring?

A) Let's not discuss climate change; what about the economy?

B) Climate change is not real because it's cold today.

C) Not all scientists agree on climate change.

D) Climate change is a natural phenomenon.

17. Identifying Main Ideas

Question 17: What is the main idea of a passage that talks about the benefits of remote work?

A) Technology is great

B) Remote work offers flexibility and work-life balance

C) Offices are outdated

D) Commuting is stressful

18. Recognizing Supporting Details

Question 18: Which of the following details would support a passage on the importance of sleep?

A) Sleeping less can lead to weight gain

B) Some people are night owls

C) Sleep is boring

D) Many people suffer from insomnia

Section 2: Writing

19. Narrative Structure

Question 19: In a narrative essay, what is the climax?

A) The highest point of tension

B) The resolution of conflicts

C) The introduction of characters

D) The initial setting

20. Emotional Appeal and Descriptive Elements

Question 20: What element can add a sense of urgency to a personal experience essay?

A) Statistics

B) Flashback

C) Rhetorical questions

D) Time constraints

21. Thesis Development

Question 21: What is a thesis statement?

A) An optional part of an essay

B) A statement that summarizes the main point

C) A question to engage readers

D) A detailed outline

22. Logical Reasoning and Evidence

Question 22: What type of evidence is most credible in an analytical essay?

A) Anecdotes

B) Expert opinions

C) Popular opinions

D) Personal experiences

Section 3: Mathematics

23. Approximations

Question 23: What is $\sqrt{50}$ rounded to the nearest whole number?

A) 6

B) 7

C) 8

D) 9

24. Data Interpretation

Question 24: If 40% of people prefer tea over coffee, what percentage of people prefer coffee?

A) 40%

B) 50%

C) 60%

D) 70%

25. Arithmetic Calculations

Question 25: What is $12 \div 4$?

A) 2

B) 3

C) 4

D) 5

26. Algebraic Equations

Question 26: What is the value of x in the equation $3x-1=5$?

A) 1

B) 2

C) 3

D) 4

27. Mathematical Relations

Question 27: If $y=2x$, what is y when $x=5$?

A) 5

B) 10

C) 15

D) 20

28. Reading Graphs and Tables

Question 28: In a pie chart representing monthly expenses, what does a larger slice mean?

A) Lower cost

B) Higher cost

C) Equal cost

D) Irrelevant information

Section 1: Reading

29. Evaluate Content

Question 29: Which of the following best supports the argument that exercise improves mental health?

A) Many people exercise daily.

B) Exercise can increase serotonin levels.

C) Exercise is hard.

D) Exercise can be fun.

30. Identify Logical Fallacies

Question 30: What is an ad hominem attack?

A) Attacking the argument directly

B) Attacking the person instead of the argument

C) Using irrelevant data

D) Overgeneralizing the situation

31. Identifying Main Ideas

Question 31: What would be the main idea of a passage about reducing plastic waste?

A) Plastic is bad.

B) Ways to reduce plastic waste for environmental sustainability.

C) Everyone uses plastic.

D) Plastic can be recycled.

32. Recognizing Supporting Details

Question 32: Which of the following would NOT support a main idea stating that regular exercise is beneficial?

A) Exercise improves cardiovascular health.

B) Exercise helps in weight loss.

C) Exercise can be time-consuming.

D) Exercise boosts mental well-being.

Section 2: Writing

33. Narrative Structure

Question 33: What is the role of the setting in a narrative essay?

A) To outline the main points

B) To provide context and mood

C) To argue a point

D) To summarize the story

34. Emotional Appeal and Descriptive Elements

Question 34: What is the purpose of using vivid language in a personal experience essay?

A) To make it longer

B) To engage the reader emotionally

C) To prove a point

D) To add complexity

35. Thesis Development

Question 35: In which part of an analytical essay would you find the thesis statement?

A) Conclusion

B) Introduction

C) Body

D) Summary

36. Logical Reasoning and Evidence

Question 36: Which of the following weakens an argument in an analytical essay?

A) Using personal anecdotes as evidence

B) Providing statistics

C) Citing expert opinions

D) Presenting facts

Section 3: Mathematics

37. Approximations

Question 37: What is the value of pi (π) rounded to the nearest tenth?

A) 3.0

B) 3.1

C) 3.2

D) 3.3

38. Data Interpretation

Question 38: If 70% of a class passed an exam, what percentage failed?

A) 20%

B) 30%

C) 40%

D) 50%

39. Arithmetic Calculations

Question 39: What is 15×3?

A) 35

B) 45

C) 55

D) 65

40. Algebraic Equations

Question 40: Solve for x in $4x+2=18$.

A) 3

B) 4

C) 5

D) 6

41. Mathematical Relations

Question 41: If $A=2B$, what is B when $A=8$?

A) 2

B) 3

C) 4

D) 5

42. Reading Graphs and Tables

Question 42: In a bar graph where the y-axis represents income and the x-axis represents age, what does a rising line indicate?

A) Income decreases with age.

B) Income increases with age.

C) Income is not related to age.

D) Age is not related to income.

Section 1: Reading

43. Evaluate Content

Question 43: Which statement would weaken an argument claiming that solar energy is completely green?

A) Solar energy relies on abundant sunlight.

B) The production of solar panels creates pollution.

C) Solar energy reduces electricity bills.

D) Solar energy can be stored for future use.

44. Identify Logical Fallacies

Question 44: What fallacy is present in the statement: "You can't be a vegetarian; you wear leather shoes!"

A) Strawman

B) Slippery Slope

C) Tu Quoque

D) Appeal to Tradition

.

45. Identifying Main Ideas

Question 45: What is the main idea of a text that discusses the benefits and drawbacks of homeschooling?

A) Homeschooling is bad.

B) Homeschooling is the best choice.

C) The advantages and disadvantages of homeschooling.

D) Schools are better than homeschooling.

46. Recognizing Supporting Details

Question 46: In an article about climate change, which of the following would be a supporting detail?

A) The opinion of a climate change denier.

B) An increase in global temperatures over the past 100 years.

C) The writer's personal experience with hot weather.

D) A quote from a fictional story about the end of the world.

Section 2: Writing

47. Narrative Structure

Question 47: What element typically comes after the climax in a narrative essay?

A) Introduction

B) Resolution

C) Rising Action

D) Conflict

48. Emotional Appeal and Descriptive Elements

Question 48: Why might an author use a metaphor in a personal experience essay?

A) To lengthen the essay

B) To provide evidence

C) To enhance emotional appeal

D) To cite a source

49. Thesis Development

Question 49: A weak thesis statement is often:

A) Specific

B) Vague

C) Arguable

D) Clear

50. Logical Reasoning and Evidence

Question 50: What type of reasoning uses specific examples to reach a general conclusion?

A) Deductive reasoning

B) Inductive reasoning

C) Circular reasoning

D) Emotional reasoning

Section 3: Mathematics

51. Approximations

Question 51: If the square root of 50 is approximately 7.071, what is it when rounded to the nearest whole number?

A) 6

B) 7

C) 8

D) 9

52. Data Interpretation

Question 52: If 50% of students like chocolate and 20% like vanilla, what percentage prefer other flavors?

A) 20%

B) 30%

C) 40%

D) 50%

53. Arithmetic Calculations

Question 53: What is $9 \div 3$?

A) 1

B) 2

C) 3

D) 4

54. Algebraic Equations

Question 54: Solve for x in $3x=12$.

A) 2

B) 3

C) 4

D) 5

55. Mathematical Relations

Question 55: Which equation represents a proportional relationship?

A) $y=2x+1$

B) $y=3x$

C) $y=x^2$

D) $y=x-2$

56. Reading Graphs and Tables

Question 56: In a pie chart that shows the time spent on daily activities, what does a larger slice indicate?

A) Less time spent on that activity.

B) More time spent on that activity.

C) The activity is more important.

D) The activity is less important.

Section 1: Reading

57. Evaluate Content

Question 57: Which of these is a credible source for a research paper on climate change?

A) An opinion blog

B) A scientific journal

C) A social media post

D) An online forum

58. Identify Logical Fallacies

Question 58: What is the logical fallacy in this statement: "If we legalize marijuana, then more dangerous drugs will also become legalized."

A) Appeal to Authority

B) Slippery Slope

C) Circular Reasoning

D) False Dichotomy

59. Identifying Main Ideas

Question 59: In a text that discusses the impact of smartphones on society, what is likely the main idea?

A) Smartphones are harmful.

B) Smartphones have an impact on society.

C) Everyone should have a smartphone.

D) Smartphones are beneficial.

60. Recognizing Supporting Details

Question 60: Which of the following would be a supporting detail in an essay arguing for solar energy?

A) A quote from a solar panel manufacturer

B) The falling cost of solar panels

C) The writer's personal switch to solar energy

D) General concerns about fossil fuels

Section 2: Writing

61. Narrative Structure

Question 61: Which element generally introduces the characters and setting in a narrative essay?

A) Climax

B) Resolution

C) Exposition

D) Rising Action

62. Emotional Appeal and Descriptive Elements

Question 62: What purpose does vivid imagery serve in a personal experience essay?

A) To confuse the reader

B) To provide factual evidence

C) To evoke emotional responses

D) To prove a logical argument

63. Thesis Development

Question 63: A strong thesis statement is:

A) Broad and general

B) Detailed and specific

C) Long and elaborate

D) Unarguable

64. Logical Reasoning and Evidence

Question 64: Which of the following provides the strongest evidence in an analytical essay?

A) Personal anecdote

B) Expert testimony

C) Common knowledge

D) A popular opinion

Section 3: Mathematics

65. Approximations

Question 65: What is the approximate square root of 60?

A) 6

B) 7

C) 8

D) 9

66. Data Interpretation

Question 66: In a class of 30 students, 10 prefer online learning. What percentage of the class prefers online learning?

A) 25%

B) 33%

C) 40%

D) 50%

67. Arithmetic Calculations

Question 67: What is 4×5?

A) 10

B) 15

C) 20

D) 25

68. Algebraic Equations

Question 68: Solve for x in $5x=25$.

A) 2

B) 4

C) 5

D) 6

69. Mathematical Relations

Question 69: What does $y=x^2$ represent?

A) A linear relationship

B) A quadratic relationship

C) An exponential relationship

D) A circular relationship

70. Reading Graphs and Tables

Question 70: In a bar graph, what does the height of the bar represent?

A) The frequency of an event

B) The area of the graph

C) The width of the data

D) The importance of the data

Section 1: Reading

71. Evaluate Content

Question 71: Which of these is NOT a credible source for academic research on history?

A) A peer-reviewed journal

B) A reputable historian's biography

C) A Wikipedia article

D) An academic textbook

72. Evaluate Content

Question 72: In a documentary about climate change, which type of content is most reliable?

A) Anecdotal stories

B) Scientific data

C) Public opinion

D) Celebrity endorsements

73. Identify Logical Fallacies

Question 73: What type of fallacy is presented in the statement, "You're either with us or against us"?

A) False Dichotomy

B) Ad Hominem

C) Strawman

D) Red Herring

74. Identify Logical Fallacies

Question 74: The claim "Everyone is buying this product, so it must be good" represents which fallacy?

A) Appeal to Ignorance

B) Appeal to Popularity

C) Circular Reasoning

D) Appeal to Authority

75. Identifying Main Ideas

Question 75: What is the main idea in an essay discussing the different types of renewable energy?

A) Solar energy is the best.

B) Renewable energy is important.

C) Renewable energy has multiple types.

D) Fossil fuels are harmful.

76. Identifying Main Ideas

Question 76: In a text about the benefits and drawbacks of remote work, what is likely the main idea?

A) Remote work is beneficial.

B) Remote work is harmful.

C) The impact of remote work is mixed.

D) Remote work is trendy.

77. Recognizing Supporting Details

Question 77: In an essay about climate change, which of these would be a supporting detail?

A) A quote from a climate scientist

B) Personal experience with hot summers

C) A popular celebrity's tweet on climate change

D) A friend's opinion about the topic

78. Recognizing Supporting Details

Question 78: Which of these would NOT be a supporting detail in an essay about the benefits of exercise?

A) Statistical data on reduced disease risks

B) Personal testimony on feeling better after exercise

C) Expert advice from a healthcare professional

D) A claim that not exercising leads to unhappiness

Section 2: Writing

79. Narrative Structure

Question 79: In a narrative essay, which element provides the conflict or challenge?

A) Exposition

B) Climax

C) Rising Action

D) Conclusion

80. Narrative Structure

Question 80: What part of a narrative essay resolves the conflict?

A) Exposition

B) Climax

C) Rising Action

D) Resolution

81. Emotional Appeal and Descriptive Elements

Question 81: Which of the following would add emotional appeal to an essay?

A) Statistics

B) Jargon

C) Personal anecdotes

D) Technical diagrams

82. Emotional Appeal and Descriptive Elements

Question 82: What is the main purpose of using descriptive elements in an essay?

A) To prove a point

B) To provide evidence

C) To evoke a sensory or emotional response

D) To make the essay longer

83. Thesis Development

Question 83: Which of the following is NOT a characteristic of a strong thesis statement?

A) It's vague and general

B) It's clear and specific

C) It takes a stance

D) It can be argued

84. Thesis Development

Question 84: In an analytical essay, where should the thesis statement typically appear?

A) In the conclusion

B) In the body paragraphs

C) In the introduction

D) It should be implied but not stated

Section 1: Reading

85. Evaluate Content

Question 85: Which source is best for researching the effects of sleep deprivation?

A) A sleep research journal

B) A lifestyle blog

C) Social media polls

D) Popular magazincs

86. Evaluate Content

Question 86: Which of these would undermine the credibility of an academic paper?

A) Citations from peer-reviewed journals

B) Extensive bibliography

C) Plagiarized content

D) In-depth analysis

87. Identify Logical Fallacies

Question 87: "If we allow students to bring smartphones to school, then they will start bringing other electronic gadgets too." What kind of logical fallacy is this?

A) Slippery Slope

B) Ad Hominem

C) Bandwagon

D) Strawman

88. Identify Logical Fallacies

Question 88: "If you care about children, you will support this policy." This statement is an example of which logical fallacy?

A) Appeal to Emotion

B) Red Herring

C) Appeal to Ignorance

D) Circular Reasoning

89. Identifying Main Ideas

Question 89: In an article discussing the harmful effects of sugar, what is likely the main idea?

A) Sugar tastes good.

B) Sugar is harmful.

C) Sugar is essential for baking.

D) Some people are allergic to sugar.

90. Identifying Main Ideas

Question 90: In a text about the benefits of meditation, what is likely the main idea?

A) Meditation is difficult.

B) Meditation is beneficial.

C) Meditation is a religious practice.

D) Meditation requires special equipment.

91. Recognizing Supporting Details

Question 91: In an article arguing for renewable energy, which would NOT be a supporting detail?

A) Economic benefits of renewable energy

B) The beauty of wind turbines

C) Environmental impact of fossil fuels

D) Scientific studies on renewable energy efficiency

92. Recognizing Supporting Details

Question 92: In a research paper about the benefits of exercise, which of these would be a supporting detail?

A) Testimonials from people who don't like to exercise

B) Data showing reduced mortality rates among regular exercisers

C) A list of popular gyms

D) The fashion aspects of workout clothes

Section 2: Writing

93. Narrative Structure

Question 93: What is the purpose of a story's exposition?

A) To introduce conflict

B) To resolve conflict

C) To set the stage for the story

D) To heighten tension

94. Narrative Structure

Question 94: In a narrative essay, which part is the climax?

A) The introduction

B) The highest point of tension

C) The resolution

D) The falling action

95. Emotional Appeal and Descriptive Elements

Question 95: Which technique can be used to add emotional depth to a personal essay?

A) Use of scientific jargon

B) First-person narration

C) Use of passive voice

D) Statistical evidence

96. Emotional Appeal and Descriptive Elements

Question 96: Which of the following elements contributes the least to the emotional appeal of an essay?

A) Anecdotal evidence

B) Personal testimony

C) Technical language

D) Descriptive details

97. Thesis Development

Question 97: What is the main function of a thesis statement in an analytical essay?

A) To summarize the entire essay

B) To introduce a counter-argument

C) To state the main argument

D) To provide supporting details

98. Logical Reasoning and Evidence

Question 98: What is the most critical component for an analytical essay to be persuasive?

A) A clear thesis

B) Logical reasoning and evidence

C) Emotional appeal

D) Beautiful language

99. Logical Reasoning and Evidence

Question 99: Which of the following is NOT a type of evidence in an analytical essay?

A) Anecdotal

B) Emotional

C) Statistical

D) Factual

100. Thesis Development

Question 100: What is a common mistake when developing a thesis for an analytical essay?

A) Being too specific

B) Being too vague

C) Including evidence

D) Including a counter-argument

4.2 ANSWER SHEET - PRACTICE TEST 1

1. Answer: B

Explanation: Statement B directly contradicts the main argument, thereby weakening it. It provides evidence that many people who eat fast food are not necessarily obese.

2. Answer: A

Explanation: An ad hominem attack targets the person rather than the argument. Option A attacks the person's education rather than addressing the argument itself.

3. Answer: B

Explanation: The main idea focuses on the environmental impact, making B the most relevant choice.

4. Answer: A

Explanation: A directly supports the topic of renewable energy by providing an attribute of solar energy, which is a type of renewable energy.

5. Answer: C

Explanation: The exposition sets the stage for the story, introducing key elements like setting, characters, and the basic situation.

6. Answer: B

Explanation: Dialogue can bring characters to life and add emotional depth to a personal experience essay.

7. Answer: B

Explanation: A good thesis statement is specific, providing a clear, concise focal point for the essay.

8. Answer: A

Explanation: Personal opinions are subjective and don't serve as reliable evidence in an analytical essay.

9. Answer: A

Explanation: π is closer to 3 than to any other whole number, so it rounds to 3.

10. Answer: B

Explanation: If 30% prefer chocolate, the remaining 70% must prefer other flavors.

11. Answer: B

Explanation: $25 \times 4 = 100$.

12. Answer: B

Explanation: Solving the equation $2x=10$, we find $x=5$.

13. Answer: A

Explanation: If $a=b$, then $a^2=b^2$.

14. Answer: C

Explanation: A descending line on a graph indicates a decrease, so the temperature must be falling.

15. Answer: A

Explanation: A provides a specific benefit of video games, thereby countering the argument that they are universally harmful.

16. Answer: A

Explanation: A red herring is an irrelevant topic introduced to divert attention from the original issue. Option A does exactly that by switching the topic to the economy.

17. Answer: B

Explanation: Option B encapsulates the central theme of a passage discussing the benefits of remote work.

18. Answer: A

Explanation: A is a detail that supports the importance of sleep by linking lack of sleep to weight gain.

19. Answer: A

Explanation: The climax is the highest point of tension or conflict in a narrative.

20. Answer: D

Explanation: Time constraints can add a sense of urgency, making the narrative more compelling.

21. Answer: B

Explanation: A thesis statement summarizes the main point or claim of the essay.

22. Answer: B

Explanation: Expert opinions provide credible and reliable evidence in an analytical essay.

23. Answer: B

Explanation: $\sqrt{50} \approx 7.0750 \approx 7.07$, which rounds to 7 when rounded to the nearest whole number.

24. Answer: C

Explanation: If 40% prefer tea, then 100% - 40% = 60% must prefer coffee.

25. Answer: B

Explanation: $12 \div 4 = 3$.

26. Answer: B

Explanation: Solving $3x-1=5$ gives $x=2$.

27. Answer: B

Explanation: If $y=2x$, then when $x=5$, $y=2\times5=10$.

28. Answer: B

Explanation: A larger slice in a pie chart indicates a higher cost or proportion of the total.

29. Answer: B

Explanation: Increasing serotonin levels directly affects mental health, making option B the best support for the argument.

30. Answer: B

Explanation: An ad hominem attack targets the person making the argument rather than the argument itself.

31. Answer: B

Explanation: Option B directly addresses the concept of reducing plastic waste and its benefit for environmental sustainability.

32. Answer: C

Explanation: Option C is a drawback of exercise and does not support the main idea that exercise is beneficial.

33. Answer: B

Explanation: The setting in a narrative essay provides context and sets the mood for the story.

34. Answer: B

Explanation: Vivid language engages the reader emotionally, adding depth to the narrative.

35. Answer: B

Explanation: The thesis statement is typically found in the introduction of an analytical essay.

36. Answer: A

Explanation: Personal anecdotes are generally considered weaker forms of evidence in an analytical context.

37. Answer: B

Explanation: The value of pi (π) is approximately 3.14159, which rounds to 3.1 when rounded to the nearest tenth.

38. Answer: B

Explanation: If 70% passed, then 100% - 70% = 30% must have failed.

39. Answer: B

Explanation: 15×3=45.

40. Answer: B

Explanation: $4x$=16 and x=4.

41. Answer: C

Explanation: If A=8, then B=2A=4.

42. Answer: B

Explanation: A rising line would indicate that income increases as age increases.

43. Answer: B

Explanation: The production of solar panels creating pollution weakens the argument that solar energy is entirely green.

44. Answer: C

Explanation: This is a Tu Quoque fallacy, which points out hypocrisy as a way to discredit an argument

45. Answer: C

Explanation: The text discusses both the benefits and drawbacks, making option C the main idea.

46. Answer: B

Explanation: An increase in global temperatures would directly support the main idea about climate change.

47. Answer: B

Explanation: The resolution usually follows the climax in a narrative structure.

48. Answer: C

Explanation: Metaphors are often used to enhance emotional appeal and depth in a narrative.

49. Answer: B

Explanation: A weak thesis statement is often vague and lacks specificity.

50. Answer: B

Explanation: Inductive reasoning moves from specific observations to broader generalizations.

51. Answer: B

Explanation: Rounded to the nearest whole number, the square root of 50 is approximately 7.

52. Answer: B

Explanation: If 50% like chocolate and 20% like vanilla, then 100% - (50% + 20%) = 30% must prefer other flavors.

53. Answer: C

Explanation: $9 \div 3 = 3$.

54. Answer: C

Explanation: $x=12/3=4$.

55. Answer: B

Explanation: In a proportional relationship, y is directly proportional to x, which is best represented by $y=3x$.

56. Answer: B

Explanation: A larger slice in a pie chart indicates more time spent on that particular activity.

57. Answer: B

Explanation: A scientific journal is a credible source for academic research on scientific topics like climate change.

58. Answer: B

Explanation: This is a Slippery Slope fallacy, assuming that one action will inevitably lead to more negative actions.

59. Answer: B

Explanation: If the text discusses the impact, both positive and negative, then the main idea is likely that smartphones have an impact on society.

60. Answer: B

Explanation: The falling cost of solar panels directly supports the argument for solar energy.

61. Answer: C

Explanation: The exposition typically introduces the characters and setting in a narrative structure.

62. Answer: C

Explanation: Vivid imagery is used to evoke emotional responses from the reader.

63. Answer: B

Explanation: A strong thesis statement is detailed and specific, providing a clear argument.

64. Answer: B

Explanation: Expert testimony provides strong, credible evidence in an analytical essay.

65. Answer: B

Explanation: The square root of 60 is approximately 7.746, which rounds to 8 when considering the nearest whole number.

66. Answer: C

Explanation: $10/30 \times 100 = 33.33$, which rounds to 33% when considering the nearest whole percentage.

67. Answer: C

Explanation: $4 \times 5 = 20$.

68. Answer: C

Explanation: $x = 25/5 = 5$.

69. Answer: B

Explanation: $y=x^2$ represents a quadratic relationship.

70. Answer: A

Explanation: The height of the bar in a bar graph generally represents the frequency of an event.

71. Answer: C

Explanation: Wikipedia, being a crowd-sourced platform, is generally not considered a credible source for academic research.

72. Answer: B

Explanation: Scientific data provides empirical evidence and is the most reliable content in a documentary about a scientific subject like climate change.

73. Answer: A

Explanation: This is a False Dichotomy fallacy, which presents an issue as having only two extremes when there may be other options.

74. Answer: B

Explanation: This is an Appeal to Popularity fallacy, suggesting that because many people do something, it must be right or good.

75. Answer: C

Explanation: If the essay discusses the different types of renewable energy, then the main idea is likely that renewable energy has multiple types.

76. Answer: C

Explanation: If the text discusses both benefits and drawbacks, then the main idea is likely that the impact of remote work is mixed.

77. Answer: A

Explanation: A quote from a climate scientist would provide credible evidence and act as a supporting detail.

78. Answer: D

Explanation: A claim that not exercising leads to unhappiness is not a direct supporting detail for the benefits of exercise and could be seen as manipulative.

79. Answer: C

Explanation: The Rising Action in a narrative essay typically introduces the conflict or challenge.

80. Answer: D

Explanation: The Resolution part of a narrative essay is where the conflict or challenge is typically resolved.

81. Answer: C

Explanation: Personal anecdotes can add emotional appeal to an essay by allowing the reader to connect with the story on a more personal level.

82. Answer: C

Explanation: Descriptive elements are used primarily to evoke a sensory or emotional response from the reader.

83. Answer: A

Explanation: A strong thesis statement should be clear, specific, and arguable, not vague and general.

84. Answer: C

Explanation: The thesis statement typically appears in the introduction of an analytical essay to give readers a clear idea of what to expect.

85. Answer: A

Explanation: A sleep research journal provides peer-reviewed and credible information, making it the best source for researching the effects of sleep deprivation.

86. Answer: C

Explanation: Plagiarized content is unethical and undermines the credibility of an academic paper.

87. Answer: A

Explanation: This is a Slippery Slope fallacy, assuming that one action will inevitably lead to a series of other actions without providing evidence.

88. Answer: A

Explanation: This is an Appeal to Emotion fallacy, attempting to manipulate the audience's feelings to gain support.

89. Answer: B

Explanation: If the article is discussing the harmful effects of sugar, then the main idea is likely that sugar is harmful.

90. Answer: B

Explanation: If the text discusses the benefits of meditation, then the main idea is likely that meditation is beneficial.

91. Answer: B

Explanation: The beauty of wind turbines would not serve as a supporting detail for the argument in favor of renewable energy.

92. Answer: B

Explanation: Data showing reduced mortality rates among regular exercisers would provide strong evidence and act as a supporting detail.

93. Answer: C

Explanation: The exposition sets the stage for the story by introducing characters, setting, and basic situational elements.

94. Answer: B

Explanation: The climax is the highest point of tension or conflict in a story.

95. Answer: B

Explanation: First-person narration allows readers to connect more deeply with the subject, adding emotional depth to the essay.

96. Answer: C

Explanation: Technical language is usually more factual and less emotive, making it the least contributory to emotional appeal.

97. Answer: C

Explanation: The thesis statement states the main argument that the rest of the essay will support or elaborate.

98. Answer: B

Explanation: Logical reasoning and evidence provide the basis for any argument, making them the most critical components for persuasiveness in an analytical essay.

99. Answer: B

Explanation: Emotional appeal is not typically considered a type of evidence in an analytical essay, which relies more on facts, data, and logical reasoning.

100. Answer: B

Explanation: A thesis that is too vague will not provide clear direction for the essay, making it difficult for the reader to understand the main argument.

5.1 FULL-LENGTH PRACTICE TEST 2

Section 1: Reading

101. Evaluate Content

Question 101: Which of the following is NOT a sign of a credible source?

A) Peer-reviewed

B) Sponsored content

C) Author's credentials are listed

D) Cites reputable sources

102. Evaluate Content

Question 102: A source that primarily uses emotionally charged language is likely:

A) Objective

B) Subjective

C) Reliable

D) Unbiased

103. Identify Logical Fallacies

Question 103: "If you don't support the proposed law, you must hate children." This statement is an example of:

A) Strawman

B) Ad hominem

C) False dilemma

D) Appeal to authority

104. Identify Logical Fallacies

Question 104: "Nine out of ten doctors recommend this brand, so it must be good." What fallacy is this?

A) Appeal to Authority

B) Slippery Slope

C) Red Herring

D) Circular Reasoning

105. Identifying Main Ideas

Question 105: What is generally the best way to identify the main idea of a passage?

A) Look for repeated terms

B) Focus on the first sentence

C) Look at the title

D) All of the above

106. Identifying Main Ideas

Question 106: In a well-organized essay, the main idea is usually found:

A) In the conclusion

B) In the introduction

C) In the body

D) Only in the title

107. Recognizing Supporting Details

Question 107: Which of the following would NOT typically serve as a supporting detail?

A) Anecdote

B) Opinion

C) Fact

D) Statistic

108. Recognizing Supporting Details

Question 108: A supporting detail is most effective when it:

A) Is subjective

B) Reinforces the main idea

C) Contradicts the main idea

D) Is unrelated to the main idea

Section 2: Writing

109. Narrative Structure

Question 109: In a narrative essay, the 'climax' usually occurs:

A) At the beginning

B) In the middle

C) Near the end

D) Right after the introduction

110. Narrative Structure

Question 110: A good narrative essay should include:

A) Dialogue

B) Emotional Appeal

C) Descriptive language

D) All of the above

111. Emotional Appeal and Descriptive Elements

Question 111: Using emotional appeal in a personal experience essay is effective for:

A) Complicating the thesis

B) Engaging the reader

C) Adding length to the essay

D) Detaching the reader from the subject

112. Emotional Appeal and Descriptive Elements

Question 112: Overusing adjectives and adverbs in a personal experience essay can make it:

A) More vivid

B) More engaging

C) Cluttered and less effective

D) More factual

113. Thesis Development

Question 113: A strong thesis statement in an analytical essay is usually:

A) A question

B) A fact

C) An opinion backed by evidence

D) A quote from a famous person

114. Thesis Development

Question 114: The thesis statement in an analytical essay should appear:

A) In the conclusion

B) In the introduction

C) In any body paragraph

D) In the footnotes

115. Logical Reasoning and Evidence

Question 115: Which is NOT a form of evidence in an analytical essay?

A) Personal anecdotes

B) Expert testimony

C) Statistical data

D) All of the above are forms of evidence

116. Logical Reasoning and Evidence

Question 116: Logical fallacies weaken an analytical essay by:

A) Making it more entertaining

B) Reducing its credibility

C) Making it longer

D) Making it more complicated

Section 3: Mathematics

117. Approximations

Question 117: If a building is approximately 200 feet tall, what is the approximate height in meters? (1 meter = 3.28084 feet)

A) 60 meters
B) 100 meters
C) 610 meters
D) 65 meters

118. Approximations

Question 118: What is π approximately equal to?

A) 3.1415
B) 3
C) 22/7
D) All of the above

119. Data Interpretation

Question 119: What does the median represent in a set of data?

A) The most frequent value
B) The middle value

C) The average

D) The range

120. Data Interpretation

Question 120: If the mean of a data set is 15, and you add a data point that is 15, what happens to the mean?

A) It stays the same

B) It decreases

C) It increases

D) Cannot be determined

121. Arithmetic Calculations

Question 121: What is 8×7?

A) 45

B) 56

C) 64

D) 60

122. Arithmetic Calculations

Question 122: What is $9 + (-3)$?

A) 12

B) 6

C) -6

D) -12

123. Algebraic Equations

Question 123: If $x=2$, what is x^2-3x+2?

A) 1

B) 2

C) 0

D) 3

124. Algebraic Equations

Question 124: Solve for x in $2x-3=5$.

A) 4

B) 3

C) 2

D) 5

125. Mathematical Relations

Question 125: If $y=3x+2$, what is y when $x=4$?

A) 14

B) 12

C) 13

D) 16

126. Mathematical Relations

Question 126: The equation $x^2-y^2=16$ is an example of:

A) Linear relation

B) Exponential relation

C) Quadratic relation

D) None of the above

127. Reading Graphs and Tables

Question 127: What does the 'y-intercept' represent in the graph of a line?

A) The slope of the line

B) The point where the line crosses the x-axis

C) The point where the line crosses the y-axis

D) The maximum value on the line

128. Reading Graphs and Tables

Question 128: In a bar graph that represents sales over time, what does the height of each bar represent?

A) Time period
B) Sales volume
C) Sales target
D) All of the above

Section 1: Reading

Critical Analysis and Evaluation

129. Evaluate Content

Question 129: What does it mean if an article has a publication date?

A) It's peer-reviewed
B) It's timely and may be more relevant
C) It's sponsored content
D) It's likely to be biased

130. Evaluate Content

Question 130: If a study is funded by a company that stands to benefit from positive results, this could lead to:

A) Impartiality
B) Bias

C) Increased credibility

D) Better research methods

131. Identify Logical Fallacies

Question 131: "If it's raining, then the ground is wet. The ground is wet. Therefore, it must be raining." What fallacy is this?

A) Slippery Slope

B) Straw Man

C) Affirming the Consequent

D) Appeal to Popularity

132. Identify Logical Fallacies

Question 132: "Everybody is doing it, so it must be right." This statement is an example of:

A) Ad Hominem

B) False Dilemma

C) Straw Man

D) Appeal to Popularity

Comprehension and Research Skills

133. Identifying Main Ideas

Question 133: What's the purpose of the topic sentence in a paragraph?

A) To provide a citation

B) To support the thesis

C) To introduce the main idea

D) To offer a conclusion

134. Identifying Main Ideas

Question 134: In an article, where is the thesis statement most likely to be found?

A) The last sentence of the article

B) The first sentence of the conclusion

C) The first paragraph

D) In the middle of the article

135. Recognizing Supporting Details

Question 135: Which of these is NOT a type of supporting detail?

A) Quotation

B) Paraphrasing

C) Opinion

D) Summary

136. Recognizing Supporting Details

Question 136: What is the role of supporting details in a paragraph?

A) To provide evidence for the main idea

B) To counter the main idea

C) To distract from the main idea

D) To repeat the main idea

Section 2: Writing

Personal Experience Essay

137. Narrative Structure

Question 137: What is the purpose of the 'setting' in a narrative essay?

A) To provide a list of characters

B) To establish the time and place of the events

C) To state the moral of the story

D) To outline the essay's main argument

138. Narrative Structure

Question 138: What is a 'denouement' in a narrative essay?

A) Introduction

B) Climax

C) Resolution

D) Conflict

139. Emotional Appeal and Descriptive Elements

Question 139: What does the 'tone' of an essay convey?

A) Author's attitude

B) Main argument

C) Textual evidence

D) Plot outline

140. Emotional Appeal and Descriptive Elements

Question 140: Using vivid imagery in a personal experience essay helps:

A) Confuse the reader

B) Engage the reader

C) Make the essay longer

D) Complicate the thesis

Analytical Essay

141. Thesis Development

Question 141: What should a thesis statement NOT be?

A) Clear

B) Debatable

C) Vague

D) Focused

142. Thesis Development

Question 142: An effective thesis statement should be:

A) A question

B) A statement

C) An exclamation

D) A quote

143. Logical Reasoning and Evidence

Question 143: Which should be avoided when presenting evidence in an analytical essay?

A) Statistics

B) Testimonials

C) Circular reasoning

D) Case studies

144. Logical Reasoning and Evidence

Question 144: Which of the following improves the credibility of an analytical essay?

A) Using jargon

B) Citing reliable sources

C) Inserting humor

D) Making assumptions

Section 3: Mathematics

Estimation, Measurement, and Statistical Principles

145. Approximations

Question 145: If a car travels 60 miles in 1 hour, approximately how far will it travel in 45 minutes?

A) 30 miles

B) 45 miles

C) 50 miles

D) 40 miles

146. Approximations

Question 146: What is the square root of 49 approximately equal to?

A) 4

B) 5

C) 7

D) 9

147. Data Interpretation

Question 147: What does the standard deviation measure in a set of data?

A) Range

B) Central tendency

C) Variability

D) Mode

148. Data Interpretation

Question 148: In a normal distribution curve, where do most data points lie?

A) At the tails

B) At the mean

C) Equally spread

D) At the median

Computation and Problem Solving

149. Arithmetic Calculations

Question 149: What is $116 \div 2$?

A) 18

B) 38

C) 48

D) 58

150. Arithmetic Calculations

Question 150: What is $5-(-2)$?

A) 7

B) 3

C) -7

D) -3

151. Algebraic Equations

Question 151: Solve for y in $3y=12$.

A) 2

B) 4

C) 5

D) 6

152. Algebraic Equations

Question 152: What is the value of y when $2y=y+1$?

A) 1

B) 2

C) 0

D) 3

Numerical and Graphic Relationships

153. Mathematical Relations

Question 153: The equation $y=x^2+2x+1$ is an example of:

A) Linear relation

B) Exponential relation

C) Quadratic relation

D) None of the above

154. Mathematical Relations

Question 154: In a coordinate plane, a line with a negative slope will:

A) Rise from left to right

B) Fall from left to right

C) Be horizontal

D) Be vertical

155. Reading Graphs and Tables

Question 155: In a bar graph, what does the height of each bar represent?

A) Frequency

B) Probability

C) Complexity

D) Length

156. Reading Graphs and Tables

Question 156: On a map, what does the 'scale' indicate?

A) Distance between two points

B) Political boundaries

C) Direction

D) Landforms

Section 1: Reading

Critical Analysis and Evaluation

157. Evaluate Content

Question 157: An article concludes that regular exercise increases happiness based on a survey where only gym-goers were interviewed. What is the main flaw in this conclusion?

A) Bias

B) Sample Size

C) Misleading Statistics

D) Complex Questioning

158. Evaluate Content

Question 158: What does an ad hominem attack do in an argument?

A) Weakens

B) Strengthens

C) Validates

D) Nullifies

159. Identify Logical Fallacies

Question 159: What does a "strawman" argument do?

A) Misrepresents

B) Validates

C) Amplifies

D) Simplifies

160. Identify Logical Fallacies

Question 160: "All lawyers are wealthy. John is a lawyer, so John is wealthy." What type of logical fallacy is this?

A) Hasty Generalization

B) Slippery Slope

C) Circular Reasoning

D) Appeal to Authority

Comprehension and Research Skills

161. Identifying Main Ideas

Question 161: What is the primary purpose of a thesis statement?

A) To summarize the main point

B) To entertain

C) To ask a question

D) To provide evidence

162. Identifying Main Ideas

Question 162: Which of these is usually found in the conclusion of an essay?

A) Hook

B) Background Information

C) Restated Thesis

D) Anecdote

163. Recognizing Supporting Details

Question 163: In a research paper, what should each paragraph primarily contain?

A) One main idea

B) Multiple main ideas

C) Only evidence

D) Counter-arguments

164. Recognizing Supporting Details

Question 164: What is the main function of a topic sentence?

A) To entertain

B) To conclude

C) To introduce the main idea

D) To provide statistical data

Section 2: Writing

Personal Experience Essay

165. Narrative Structure

Question 165: In a narrative essay, what role does the climax play?

A) Introduction

B) Resolution

C) Highest Point of Tension

D) Background Information

166. Narrative Structure

Question 166: What does the "resolution" in a narrative essay provide?

A) Conflict

B) Closure

C) Introduction

D) Suspense

167. Emotional Appeal and Descriptive Elements

Question 167: What does "pathos" appeal to?

A) Logic

B) Emotion

C) Ethics

D) None of the above

168. Emotional Appeal and Descriptive Elements

Question 168: What is the main function of descriptive language?

A) To argue

B) To inform

C) To entertain

D) To create a vivid picture

Analytical Essay

169. Thesis Development

Question 169: Which of the following best describes a "counterargument"?

A) An argument that supports the thesis

B) An argument that opposes the thesis

C) An irrelevant argument

D) A clarifying argument

170. Thesis Development

Question 170: What is the main purpose of the "hook" in an analytical essay?

A) To present the thesis

B) To grab the reader's attention

C) To provide evidence

D) To summarize the conclusion

171. Logical Reasoning and Evidence

Question 171: What type of evidence is least effective in an analytical essay?

A) Anecdotal

B) Statistical

C) Expert Testimony

D) Empirical

172. Logical Reasoning and Evidence

Question 172: Which of these is not a type of logical fallacy?

A) Red Herring

B) Straw Man

C) Bandwagon

D) Quantitative Data

Section 3: Mathematics

Estimation, Measurement, and Statistical Principles

173. Approximations

Question 173: What does it mean if a measurement is "accurate"?

A) Precise

B) Close to the true value

C) Repeatedly Consistent

D) Rounded Off

174. Approximations

Question 174: When estimating a large number, what is commonly used?

A) Pi

B) Square Root

C) Rounding

D) Division

175. Data Interpretation

Question 175: In a histogram, what does the width of each bar represent?

A) Count

B) Frequency

C) Data Range

D) Percentage

176. Data Interpretation

Question 176: What does the median represent in a data set?

A) Average

B) Most Common Value

C) Middle Value

D) Range

Computation and Problem Solving

177. Arithmetic Calculations

Question 177: What is 13^2?

A) 119
B) 129
C) 149
D) 169

178. Arithmetic Calculations

Question 178: What is the result of $10-4\times2$?

A) 12
B) 2
C) 4
D) 6

179. Algebraic Equations

Question 179: What is the value of x in the equation $2x=16$?

A) 4
B) 8
C) 6
D) 32

180. Algebraic Equations

Question 180: Solve for x in $3x-4=11$.

A) 3

B) 5

C) 6

D) 8

Numerical and Graphic Relationships

181. Mathematical Relations

Question 181: If $y=2x+1$, what is y when $x=3$?

A) 5

B) 7

C) 9

D) 10

182. Mathematical Relations

Question 182: Which of these equations represents a straight line?

A) $y=x^2$

B) $y=3x+2$

C) $y=\sin(x)$

D) $y=\log(x)$

183. Reading Graphs and Tables

Question 183: What does the y-intercept in a graph usually represent?

A) Slope

B) Starting Point

C) Range

D) Frequency

184. Reading Graphs and Tables

Question 184: In a pie chart, what does each slice represent?

A) Total Quantity

B) A percentage of the whole

C) Relative frequency

D) None of the above

Section 1: Reading

Critical Analysis and Evaluation

185. Evaluate Content

Question 185: When presented with a fact-based article, which of the following should you NOT do?

A) Verify the facts
B) Check the source
C) Rely solely on your opinion
D) Consider alternative viewpoints

186. Evaluate Content

Question 186: What is the primary objective of a persuasive essay?

A) To entertain
B) To inform
C) To persuade
D) To explain

187. Identify Logical Fallacies

Question 187: What is an Ad Hominem fallacy?

A) Attacking the argument
B) Attacking the person
C) Using irrelevant data
D) Using circular reasoning

188. Identify Logical Fallacies

Question 188: What does a "Slippery Slope" fallacy entail?

A) A single cause leading to multiple effects

B) An argument based on fear

C) Sequential events leading to an extreme conclusion

D) Arguing without evidence

Comprehension and Research Skills

189. Identifying Main Ideas

Question 189: What does a thesis statement do?

A) Summarizes the article

B) Outlines the supporting details

C) Expresses the main idea

D) Provides background information

190. Identifying Main Ideas

Question 190: What should the introduction of an article contain?

A) Summary

B) Conclusion

C) Main idea

D) Supporting details

191. Recognizing Supporting Details

Question 191: What role do examples play in a text?

A) Contradict the main idea

B) Support the main idea

C) Summarize the main idea

D) Replace the main idea

192. Recognizing Supporting Details

Question 192: Which of the following is NOT a supporting detail?

A) Fact

B) Statistic

C) Opinion

D) Example

Section 2: Writing

Personal Experience Essay

193. Narrative Structure

Question 193: What is the climax of a story?

A) Beginning

B) Tension peak

C) Conclusion

D) Background

194. Narrative Structure

Question 194: What element adds depth to a character in a story?

A) Simplicity

B) Complexity

C) Predictability

D) Consistency

195. Emotional Appeal and Descriptive Elements

Question 195: What is pathos?

A) Ethical appeal

B) Logical appeal

C) Emotional appeal

D) Humorous appeal

196. Emotional Appeal and Descriptive Elements

Question 196: What role does imagery play in writing?

A) To complicate the text

B) To clarify the text

C) To evoke sensory experiences

D) To provide statistics

197. Thesis Development

Question 197: What is the first step in developing a thesis?

A) Writing the conclusion

B) Conducting research

C) Understanding the topic

D) Drafting the introduction

198. Thesis Development

Question 198: What is a counter-argument?

A) Supporting argument

B) Neutral argument

C) Opposing argument

D) Irrelevant argument

199. Logical Reasoning and Evidence

Question 199: What is an inductive argument?

A) From specific to general

B) From general to specific

C) Circular reasoning

D) Either A or B

200. Logical Reasoning and Evidence

Question 200: What is a syllogism?

A) Fallacy

B) Anecdote

C) Form of deductive reasoning

D) Metaphor

5.2 ANSWER SHEET - PRACTICE TEST 2

101. Answer: B

Explanation: Sponsored content may introduce bias and is not necessarily credible.

102. Answer: B

Explanation: Emotionally charged language often signals a subjective or biased perspective.

103. Answer: C

Explanation: This is a false dilemma, presenting only two options when there may be more.

104. Answer: A

Explanation: This is an appeal to authority, relying on the expertise of others as the sole basis of the argument.

105. Answer: D

Explanation: All these methods can be useful in identifying the main idea.

106. Answer: B

Explanation: The introduction typically presents the main idea to guide the reader.

107. Answer: B

Explanation: An opinion by itself does not serve as a supporting detail without evidence or reasoning.

108. Answer: B

Explanation: A supporting detail should reinforce the main idea for it to be effective.

109. Answer: C

Explanation: The climax is generally near the end, resolving the main conflict or point of tension.

110. Answer: D

Explanation: A well-rounded narrative essay could benefit from all these elements.

111. Answer: B

Explanation: Emotional appeal can make the essay more relatable and engaging for the reader.

112. Answer: C

Explanation: Overuse can make the essay cluttered and detract from its effectiveness.

113. Answer: C

Explanation: A strong thesis is an opinion or argument that can be backed up with evidence.

114. Answer: B

Explanation: The thesis generally appears in the introduction to guide the reader.

115. Answer: A

Explanation: Personal anecdotes are generally not considered strong evidence in an analytical essay.

116. Answer: B

Explanation: Logical fallacies can undermine an argument's credibility.

117. Answer: A

Explanation: ≈200 feet/3.28084≈61 meters, which is closest to 60 meters.

118. Answer: D

Explanation: All options are common approximations for π.

119. Answer: B

Explanation: The median is the middle value in a sorted data set.

120. Answer: A

Explanation: Adding a data point equal to the mean will not change the mean.

121. Answer: B

Explanation: 8×7=56.

122. Answer: B

Explanation: $9+(-3)=6$.

123. Answer: C

Explanation: $x^2-3x+2=4-6+2=0$.

124. Answer: A

Explanation: $2x=8$, $x=4$.

125. Answer: A

Explanation: $y=3\times4+2=14$.

126. Answer: C

Explanation: Both x and y are squared, making it a quadratic relation.

127. Answer: C

Explanation: The y-intercept is the point at which the line crosses the y-axis.

128. Answer: B

Explanation: The height of each bar usually represents the sales volume for that time period.

129. Answer: B

Explanation: A publication date often indicates timeliness and can help readers assess the relevance of the content.

130. Answer: B

Explanation: Funding from a company with a vested interest could introduce bias into the study's results.

131. Answer: C

Explanation: This is affirming the consequent, a logical fallacy where the conclusion does not follow logically from the premises.

132. Answer: D

Explanation: This is an appeal to popularity, suggesting that popularity alone validates an action or idea.

133. Answer: C

Explanation: The topic sentence introduces the main idea of the paragraph.

134. Answer: C

Explanation: The thesis statement is generally found in the first paragraph to set the tone and direction for the article.

135. Answer: C

Explanation: Opinion, by itself, does not act as a supporting detail unless backed by evidence or reasoning.

136. Answer: A

Explanation: Supporting details provide evidence or examples to substantiate the main idea of a paragraph.

137. Answer: B

Explanation: The setting establishes the time and place where the events in the narrative occur.

138. Answer: C

Explanation: The denouement is the resolution or conclusion of the narrative.

139. Answer: A

Explanation: The tone of an essay communicates the author's attitude toward the subject matter or the audience.

140. Answer: B

Explanation: Vivid imagery can make the narrative more engaging and relatable.

141. Answer: C

Explanation: A thesis statement should be clear, focused, and debatable; it should not be vague.

142. Answer: B

Explanation: An effective thesis statement is generally a declarative statement that guides the essay.

143. Answer: C

Explanation: Circular reasoning is a fallacy and weakens your argument.

144. Answer: B

Explanation: Citing reliable sources improves the credibility of an essay by providing verifiable evidence or expert opinions.

145. Answer: B

Explanation: 45 minutes is 3/4 of an hour, and 3/4 of 60 miles is 45 miles.

146. Answer: C

Explanation: $\sqrt{49}=7$.

147. Answer: C

Explanation: Standard deviation measures the variability or dispersion in a set of data.

148. Answer: B

Explanation: In a normal distribution, most data points cluster around the mean.

149. Answer: D

Explanation: $116 \div 2 = 58$.

150. Answer: A

Explanation: $5-(-2)=5+2=7$.

151. Answer: B

Explanation: $3y=12$, $y=4$.

152. Answer: A

Explanation: $2y=y+1$, $y=1$.

153. Answer: C

Explanation: The equation contains an x^2 term, making it a quadratic relation.

154. Answer: B

Explanation: A line with a negative slope will fall as it moves from left to right.

155. Answer: A

Explanation: The height of each bar typically represents the frequency or count of data points for that category.

156. Answer: A

Explanation: The scale on a map indicates the proportionate distance between two points in the real world.

157. Answer: A

Explanation: The survey has a biased sample, as it only interviews people who go to the gym.

158. Answer: A

Explanation: An ad hominem attack weakens an argument by attacking the character of a person rather than the issue at hand.

159. Answer: A

Explanation: A strawman argument misrepresents the opponent's position to make it easier to attack.

160. Answer: A

Explanation: This is a hasty generalization, as it makes an overbroad claim based on limited evidence.

161. Answer: A

Explanation: The primary purpose of a thesis statement is to summarize the main point of an essay or article.

162. Answer: C

Explanation: A restated thesis is often found in the conclusion to remind the reader of the main point.

163. Answer: A

Explanation: Each paragraph should primarily contain one main idea supported by evidence and analysis.

164. Answer: C

Explanation: The main function of a topic sentence is to introduce the main idea of the paragraph.

165. Answer: C

Explanation: The climax is the highest point of tension or conflict in a narrative essay.

166. Answer: B

Explanation: The resolution provides closure by resolving the conflict and tying up loose ends.

167. Answer: B

Explanation: Pathos appeals to the emotions of the audience.

168. Answer: D

Explanation: The main function of descriptive language is to create a vivid picture in the reader's mind.

169. Answer: B

Explanation: A counterargument is an argument that opposes the thesis but is addressed to strengthen your own position.

170. Answer: B

Explanation: The main purpose of the "hook" is to grab the reader's attention right at the beginning.

171. Answer: A

Explanation: Anecdotal evidence is generally considered the least effective because it is subjective and not always universally applicable.

172. Answer: D

Explanation: Quantitative data is a type of evidence, not a logical fallacy.

173. Answer: B

Explanation: An accurate measurement is one that is close to the true or actual value.

174. Answer: C

Explanation: Rounding is commonly used when estimating a large number to make it more manageable.

175. Answer: C

Explanation: The width of each bar in a histogram represents the data range for that specific bar.

176. Answer: C

Explanation: The median is the middle value in a data set when it is organized in ascending or descending order.

177. Answer: D

Explanation: 13^2 or 13 squared is 169.

178. Answer: B

Explanation: Following the order of operations, $10-4\times2=10-8=2$.

179. Answer: B

Explanation: $2x=16\Longrightarrow x=8$.

180. Answer: B

Explanation: $3x-4=11\Longrightarrow3x=15\Longrightarrow x=5$.

181. Answer: B

Explanation: $y=2x+1\Longrightarrow y=2\times3+1=7$.

182. Answer: B

Explanation: $y=3x+2$ represents a straight line, as it is in the form $y=mx+b$.

183. Answer: B

Explanation: The y-intercept is usually the starting point or initial condition of a situation modeled by the graph.

184. Answer: B

Explanation: Each slice in a pie chart represents a percentage of the whole data set or category.

185. Answer: C

Explanation: Relying solely on your opinion doesn't contribute to a critical evaluation of the content.

186. Answer: C

Explanation: The primary objective of a persuasive essay is to persuade the reader to a specific viewpoint.

187. Answer: B

Explanation: An Ad Hominem fallacy involves attacking the character of the person rather than their argument.

188. Answer: C

Explanation: A "Slippery Slope" fallacy involves a series of events that lead to an extreme conclusion, often without proper justification.

189. Answer: C

Explanation: A thesis statement expresses the main idea or argument of the essay or article.

190. Answer: C

Explanation: The introduction should introduce the main idea or thesis of the article.

191. Answer: B

Explanation: Examples in a text serve to support the main idea or thesis.

192. Answer: C

Explanation: An opinion is not necessarily a supporting detail unless it is backed by facts or data.

193. Answer: B

Explanation: The climax is the moment when the tension or conflict reaches its peak.

194. Answer: B

Explanation: Complexity adds depth to a character, making them more interesting and relatable.

195. Answer: C

Explanation: Pathos is an appeal to the audience's emotions.

196. Answer: C

Explanation: Imagery is used to evoke sensory experiences and create a vivid picture in the reader's mind.

197. Answer: C

Explanation: Understanding the topic is the first step, as it lays the foundation for research and thesis development.

198. Answer: C

Explanation: A counter-argument is an argument that opposes the thesis or main argument.

199. Answer: A

Explanation: An inductive argument reasons from specific instances to a general conclusion.

200. Answer: C

Explanation: A syllogism is a form of deductive reasoning consisting of a major premise, a minor premise, and a conclusion.

TEST-TAKING STRATEGIES

Navigating the CBEST with Confidence

Test-Taking Strategies

1. Time Management Mastery

- **Prioritize Questions:** Quickly assess the difficulty of each question. Answer the ones you find easier first, then revisit the more challenging ones.

- **Set Time Limits:** Allocate a specific amount of time to each section and question. Stick to these limits to ensure you cover all questions effectively.

2. Strategic Guessing

- **Eliminate Wrong Choices:** Use the process of elimination to identify and eliminate obviously incorrect options, increasing your chances of guessing the correct answer.

- **Educated Guessing:** When unsure, make an educated guess by considering context, eliminating extremes, and leveraging any partial knowledge.

3. Effective Reading Techniques

- **Skim Passages:** Quickly read through passages to grasp the main idea before diving into the questions. This approach helps you locate relevant information more efficiently.

- **Highlight Key Phrases:** Use highlighting strategically. Mark key phrases or details that are likely to be crucial for answering questions.

4. Essay Planning

- **Organize Thoughts:** Before diving into writing, spend a few minutes planning your essay. Outline key points and ensure a logical flow of ideas for a well-structured response.

- **Time Allocation:** Divide your time wisely between planning, writing, and revising. Ensure you have sufficient time for each phase of the essay.

Overcoming Test Anxiety

1. Breathing Techniques

- **Deep Breaths:** Practice deep, slow breaths to calm your nervous system. Inhale deeply through your nose, hold for a few seconds, and exhale slowly through your mouth.

- **Focus on Breathing Patterns:** Develop a rhythm that works for you. Use this technique during breaks or whenever you feel anxiety rising.

2. Positive Visualization

- **Visualize Success:** Close your eyes and visualize yourself confidently answering questions and completing the exam. Positive visualization can enhance your self-belief.

- **Create a Relaxing Mental Image:** Imagine a calming place or scenario. This mental escape can help reduce stress during the exam.

3. Mindfulness Techniques

- **Focus on the Present:** Practice mindfulness by bringing your attention to the present moment. Concentrate on the task at hand rather than anticipating future challenges.

- **Body Scan:** Perform a quick body scan to identify and release tension. This helps maintain a relaxed state of mind.

4. Pre-Exam Rituals

- **Establish a Routine:** Develop pre-exam rituals that help you relax. This could include a brief walk, listening to calming music, or engaging in a few minutes of light stretching.

- **Positive Affirmations:** Repeat positive affirmations to boost your confidence. Remind yourself of your preparation and capabilities.

Your Roadmap to Success

Mastering these test-taking strategies and overcoming test anxiety is your roadmap to success in the CBEST. As you apply these techniques, remember that confidence and preparation go hand in hand. You've got this!

ADDITIONAL RESOURCES

Enhance Your Preparation with Comprehensive Resources

Recommended Online Resources

1. CBEST Official Website

- **Link:** CBEST Official Website

- **Why:** Access official information about the CBEST exam, including test dates, registration details, and official practice materials.

2. Khan Academy

- **Link:** Khan Academy - CBEST Preparation

- **Why:** Khan Academy offers a variety of instructional videos and practice exercises to reinforce your understanding of key concepts tested in the CBEST.

3. Quizlet

- **Link:** Quizlet - CBEST Flashcards

- **Why:** Explore a collection of CBEST flashcards created by educators and students. Engage in interactive learning to reinforce your knowledge.

4. Magoosh

- **Link:** Magoosh - CBEST Study Resources

- **Why:** Magoosh provides comprehensive study resources, including video lessons, practice questions, and study schedules to supplement your preparation.

Recommended Academic Materials

1. CliffsNotes CBEST

- **Available at:** CliffsNotes CBEST

- **Why:** The CliffsNotes CBEST guide offers concise reviews of key topics, practice tests, and helpful strategies to enhance your preparation.

2. Barron's CBEST

- **Available at:** Barron's CBEST

- **Why:** Barron's CBEST guide provides in-depth content reviews, practice tests, and expert tips to ensure a comprehensive understanding of the exam.

3. Princeton Review: Cracking the CBEST

- **Available at:** Princeton Review - CBEST

- **Why:** The Princeton Review guide offers proven strategies, practice tests, and targeted content reviews to help you excel on the CBEST.

Tailoring Your Approach

While "CBEST Prep Book 2023-2024" serves as your primary guide, these recommended online resources and academic materials provide additional support and diverse perspectives to enrich your preparation. Tailor your approach by exploring these resources based on your learning preferences and needs.

FINAL WORDS

YOUR JOURNEY TO SUCCESS

Embracing the Future with Confidence

Dear Future Educators,

As you reach the end of your preparation journey with "CBEST Prep Book 2023-2024," we want to share a few words of encouragement and motivation. The path you've embarked on is not just about passing a test; it's about realizing your potential and shaping a future filled with endless opportunities.

The Power of Perseverance

Throughout this journey, you've demonstrated resilience and dedication. Remember that every challenge you've faced in your preparation has been a stepping stone toward your goal. Perseverance is your greatest ally, and it will carry you through the moments of uncertainty.

Believe in Your Abilities

As you sit down to take the CBEST, trust in the knowledge you've acquired and the skills you've honed. You are more than capable of overcoming any challenge that comes your way. Believe in your abilities, and let your confidence shine through in every response.

It's More Than a Test

The CBEST is a milestone, but it's not the final destination. This journey is a testament to your passion for education and your commitment to making a difference. Use the knowledge gained not only to succeed in the exam but to thrive in your future classrooms.

Opportunities Await

Beyond the test results lie opportunities waiting to be seized. Whether it's shaping young minds, igniting curiosity, or fostering a love for learning, you have the power to make a lasting impact. Embrace the challenges and joys that come with being an educator.

Your Success Inspires Others

Your success is not just a personal achievement; it's an inspiration to others who aspire to follow in your footsteps. Share your journey, offer support, and contribute to a community driven by the pursuit of knowledge and excellence.

The Journey Continues

As you turn the last page of "CBEST Prep Book 2023-2024," remember that your journey in education is ongoing. Keep seeking knowledge, embracing growth, and nurturing your passion for learning. The world awaits the impact only you can make.

Best Wishes on Your CBEST Journey

EXPLORE OUR RANGE OF STUDY GUIDES

At Test Treasure Publication, we understand that academic success requires more than just raw intelligence or tireless effort—it requires targeted preparation. That's why we offer an extensive range of study guides, meticulously designed to help you excel in various exams across the USA.

Our Offerings

- **Medical Exams:** Conquer the MCAT, USMLE, and more with our comprehensive study guides, complete with practice questions and diagnostic tests.

- **Law Exams:** Get a leg up on the LSAT and bar exams with our tailored resources, offering theoretical insights and practical exercises.

- **Business and Management Tests:** Ace the GMAT and other business exams with our incisive guides, equipped with real-world examples and scenarios.

- **Engineering & Technical Exams:** Prep for the FE, PE, and other technical exams with our specialized guides, which delve into both fundamentals and complexities.

- **High School Exams:** Be it the SAT, ACT, or AP tests, our high school range is designed to give you a competitive edge.

- **State-Specific Exams:** Tailored resources to help you with exams unique to specific states, whether it's teacher qualification exams or state civil service exams.

Why Choose Test Treasure Publication?

- **Comprehensive Coverage:** Each guide covers all essential topics in detail.

- **Quality Material:** Crafted by experts in each field.

- **Interactive Tools:** Flashcards, online quizzes, and downloadable resources to complement your study.

- **Customizable Learning:** Personalize your prep journey by focusing on areas where you need the most help.

- **Community Support:** Access to online forums where you can discuss concerns, seek guidance, and share success stories.

Contact Us

For inquiries about our study guides, or to provide feedback, please email us at support@testtreasure.com.

Order Now

Ready to elevate your preparation to the next level? Visit our website www.testtreasure.com to browse our complete range of study guides and make your purchase.

Made in the USA
Las Vegas, NV
02 June 2024

90622686R00090